# Introducing Islam to Non-Muslims

by

**Ahmad Hussein Sakr**
And
**Hussein Khalid Al-Hussein**

**Islamic Book Service (P) Ltd.**

# Introducing Islam to No-Muslims

**by Ahmed Hussein Sakr & Hussein Khalid Al-Hussein**

**ISBN 81-7231-311-X**

**First Edition : 2001**
**Reprint : 2012**

**Published by**

**Islamic Book Service (P) Ltd.**

2872-74, Kucha Chelan, Darya Ganj,
**New Delhi**-110002 **(India)**
**Ph.:** 011-23253514, 23269050, 23286551
**Fax:** 011-23277913 | **Email:** islamic@eth.net
**Website:** www.islamicbookservice.co

**Our Associates**

- Al-Munna Book Shop Ltd. **(U.A.E.)**
  **(Sharjah)** ***Tel.:*** 06-561-5483, 06-561-4650
  **(Dubai)** ***Tel.:*** 04-352-9294
- Azhar Academy Ltd., **London (United Kingdom)**
  ***Tel.:*** 020-8911-9797
- Lautan Lestari (Lestari Books), **Jakarta (Indonesia)**
  ***Tel.:*** 0062-21-35-23456
- Husami Book Depot, **Hyderabad (India)**
  ***Tel.:*** 040-6680-6285

**Printed in India**

## DEDICATION

This booklet is dedicated for the pleasure of Allah (swt), and for the love of His Prophet and last Messenger Muhammad (pbuh).

## SPECIAL DU'A

*We pray to Allah(swt) to bless all the members of the family of the Prophet, and to reward all the companions of the Prophet, especially those who assumed the responsibility of being Khulafa' Rashidun. We pray to Allah(swt) to reward all the Ulama' who delivered the Message of Allah and all of those who taught Islam to the authors of this manuscript including their parents,Ameen.*

# Arabic Letters

**The following system has been used in transliterating some Arabic letters to English:**

| Arabic | Name | Sound | English Example |
|---|---|---|---|
| ء | hamzah | ’ | America |
| ث | thā | th | thick |
| ح | ḥā | ḥ | |
| خ | khā | kh | |
| ذ | ẓāl | ẓ | this |
| ص | ṣād | ṣ | bus |
| ض | dhād | dh | mud |
| ط | ṭā | ṭ | Boston |
| ظ | ẓā | ẓ | |
| ع | ‘ayn | ‘ | |
| غ | ghayn | gh | |
| ق | q̣āf | q̣ | |
| ا | aleph | ā | art |
| و | wow | ū | tooth |
| ي | yā | ī | feel |
| ـَ | fatḥah | a | temporary |
| ـُ | dhammah | u | temporary |
| ـِ | kasrah | i | liquid |

# Preface

**{{In the name of Allāh, the Beneficent, the Merciful}}**

**{{*Call unto the way of your Lord with wisdom and fair exhortation, and reason with them in the better way. Lo! your Lord is best aware of those who stray from His way, and He is best aware of those who go aright.*}} *[Al-Qur'ān: An-Naḥl (16:125)].***

**This booklet is written to familiarize the reader with the basic concepts of Islām and the main glossaries and expressions used by Muslims throughout the world. It is mainly written for non-Muslims to familiarize them with the basic concepts of the Islāmic faith and Islāmic terminology, but it can also be helpful for Muslims as well.**

**Although it is very hard to explain Islām in one book, there is always a need for a short document on Islām for the readers who do not have the time to read larger books. Those who like to peruse further reading about Islām in English will find the recommended books at the end of this booklet very helpful.**

**This manuscript is also designed to build and to establish a bridge of understanding between Muslims and non-Muslims. It is only through communication and proper exchange of information that people will understand the culture, faith, and creed of one another. It is written with that understanding as an eye-opener to both groups of Muslims and non-Muslims. This manuscript has been prepared in three chapters, namely: ABC's of Islām, Islāmic Glossaries, and Islāmic Expressions.**

**We pray to Almighty *Allāh* (God) to accept this humble effort and to forgive our shortcomings. {{*Our Lord! Do not condemn ·t we forget or miss the mark!*}} *[Al-Qur'ān: Al-Baqarah (2:286)].* {{*Our Lord! Accept from us. Lo! You, only You, are the Hearer, the Knower.*}} *[Al-Qur'ān: Al-Baqarah (2:127)].***

**Ḥussein Khālid Al-Ḥussein and Dr. Aḥmad Ṣaqr**

# Contents

# Chapter 1

# ABC'S OF ISLĀM

## 1.1 Islām and Muslims

Islām is the name of the religion that Muslims believe in. In some parts of the world, two terminologies have been used to identify Islām and Muslims, namely: Mohammedanism and Mohammedans. These two words are considered to be misnomers as they give wrong impressions about Islām and Muslims. One may think that the founder of Islām was Prophet Muḥammad (s.a.w.), while the founder of Islām is *Allāh*, Almighty God, the Creator of the Universe. One may also think that the religion of Islām has taken its name after a mortal person such as Muḥammad himself (s.a.w.); and that Islām is no more than another 'ISM' just like Judaism, Hinduism, Marxism, Socialism, Arabism, Nationalism, etc. The word Mohammedans may also make people think that Muslims are worshipers of Muḥammad (s.a.w.) or believers in him in the same way as Christians believe in Jesus. All these interpretations are wrong and misleading.

The name of this religion is Islām, the root of which is *Silm* and *Salām* which means peace. *Salām* may also mean greeting one another with peace. One of the beautiful names of *Allāh* is that He is the Peace. Islām means purity and submission to *Allāh*, the One God, and to live in peace with the Creator, within one's self, and with other people, the environment, and the whole Universe. Thus, Islām is a total system of living. A Muslim is supposed to live in peace and harmony with all these segments; hence, a Muslim is any person anywhere in the world whose obedience, allegiance, and loyalty are to *Allāh*, the Lord of the Universe.

## 1.2 Muslims and Arabs

The followers of Islām are called Muslims. Muslims are not to be confused with Arabs. Muslims may be Arabs, Turks, Persians, Indians, Pakistanis, Malaysians, Indonesians, Europeans, Africans, Americans, or may be from any other nationality.

An Arab could be a Muslim, a Christian, a Jew, an agnostic, or an atheist. Any person who adopts the Arabic language is called an Arab. Nevertheless, the language of the *Qur'ān* (the Holy Book of Islām) is Arabic. Muslims all over the world try to learn Arabic so that they may be able to read the *Qur'ān* and understand its meanings. They pray in the language of the *Qur'ān*, namely Arabic. Supplications to *Allāh* could be in any language.

While there are one billion Muslims in the world there are about 200 million Arabs. Among the Arabs, about ten percent are not Muslims. Hence, Arab Muslims constitute only about twenty percent of the Muslim population of the world.

## 1.3 Allāh the One and Only God

*Allāh* is the name of the One and Only God. The *Qur'ān* mentions ninety-nine beautiful names for *Allāh* such as: The Gracious, The Merciful, The Beneficent, The Creator, The All-Knowing, The All-Wise, The Lord of the Universe, The First, The Last, and others.

*Allāh* is the Creator of all human beings. He is the God for the Christians, the Jews, the Muslims, the Buddhists, the Hindus, the atheists, and all human beings, whether they believe in Him or not. Muslims worship *Allāh*, put their trust in Him, and seek His help and His guidance.

The right belief in the attributes of *Allāh* means that people should not deny any of such attributes, nor should they try to think of what He looks like. For instance, Muslims should believe that He has eyes and hands, as mentioned in the *Qur'ān*, but they should not try to make analogy between His hands and eyes and the human hands and eyes, nor should they deny the presence of real hands and eyes for *Allāh*.

Muslims do not believe that human beings are in the image of *Allāh*. The *Qur'ān* says: {{*Naught is as His likeness*}} *[Al-Qur'ān: Ash-Shūrā (42:11)]*.

## 1.4 Muḥammad (s.a.w.)

Muḥammad (s.a.w.) was chosen by *Allāh* to deliver His Message of Peace, namely Islām. He was born in 570 C.E. (Common Era), in Makkah, a city in Arabia. At the age of forty, he was entrusted with the Message of Islām. The revelation that he received is called the *Qur'ān*, while the message is called Islām.

Muḥammad (s.a.w.) is the very last prophet of *Allāh* to mankind. He is the final Messenger of *Allāh*. His message was and is still to the Christians, the Jews, and the rest of mankind. He was sent to those religious people to inform them about the true mission of Jesus, Moses, David, Jacob, Isaac, and Abraham.

Muḥammad (s.a.w.) is considered to be the summation and the culmination of all the prophets and Messengers that came before him. He purified the previous messages from adulteration, and completed the Message of *Allāh* to all humanities. He was entrusted with the power of explaining, interpreting, and living the teachings of the *Qur'ān*.

## 1.5 Sources of Islām

The legal sources of Islām are the *Qur'ān* and the *Sunnah*. The *Qur'ān* is the exact words of *Allāh*; its authenticity, originality, and totality are intact. Whoever is interested to find out the originality and the purity of Christianity and Judaism may indeed find them directly in the *Qur'ān*.

The language of the *Qur'ān* is Arabic. It can't be translated to any language. Whenever it is translated, it is no more the *Qur'ān*. It loses its beauty, its spirituality, and its being the words of *Allāh*. The translation gives only the meaning and cannot be considered *Qur'ān*.

The translation also makes some expressions and words lose some of their meanings when they have more than one meaning in Arabic or when their exact interpretation is not known yet, as is the case in translating the scientific references in the *Qur'ān*. However, the meanings of the verses that are necessary for one's belief can all be translated, which makes it possible for anybody to understand or accept the belief of Islām, even before learning Arabic.

The *Qur'ān* is memorized by millions of Muslims throughout the world. While reciting it, one feels its beauty of eloquence, rhyme, rhythm, and melody.

The *Sunnah* is the report of the sayings, deeds, and approvals of Prophet Muḥammad (s.a.w.). The sayings and deeds of the Prophet (s.a.w.) are called *Sunnah*.

The *Sīrah* is the writings of scholars of Islām about the life of the Prophet (s.a.w.). Hence, it is the life history of Prophet Muḥammad (s.a.w.) which provides examples of daily living for Muslims.

## 1.6 Some Islāmic Principles

*Allāh* instructed Muslims to have faith and to believe in some major principles. These are specific and general values that are based on universal standards, irrespective of color, nationality, race, sex, ethnic background, or position. Some of these principles are included in this section.

### 1.6.1 Oneness of God

*Allāh* is the One and the Only God. He is the only creator of everything, and Muslims do worship Him. He is not two in one, three in one, or one in three. This means that Islām rejects the idea of trinity or such a unity of God, which implies more than one god in one. The *Qur'ān* mentions ninety-nine beautiful names and attributes for *Allāh*. Through the names and attributes of *Allāh* Muslims recognize Him, appreciate His favors, and understand their duties toward Him, and His responsibilities for the whole Universe.

### 1.6.2 Oneness of Mankind

People are created equal in front of the Law of *Allāh*. There is no superiority for one race over another. Men and women are equally responsible to *Allāh*. *Allāh* made us of different colors, nationalities, languages, genders, and beliefs so as to test who is going to be better than others. It is only *Allāh* Himself who knows the best. It depends on righteousness and piety.

People are not to be judged on factors that they had no choice of such as gender, color, size, looks, race, or health. The *Qur'ān* says: {{*O mankind! Lo! We have created you from male and female, and have made you nations and tribes that you may know one another. Lo! the noblest of you, in the sight of Allāh, is the best in obeying Allāh. Lo! Allāh is Knower, Aware.*}} *[Al-Qur'ān: Al-Ḥujurāt (49:13)]*.

### 1.6.3 Oneness of the Message and Messengers

Muslims believe that *Allāh* sent different messengers throughout the history of mankind. All came with the same message and the same teachings. It was the people who misunderstood and misinterpreted them.

Muslims believe in all the prophets of *Allāh* like Noah, Abraham, Isaac, Ishmael, Jacob, Moses, David, Jesus, and Muḥammad (s.a.w.). The prophets of Judaism and Christianity are indeed the prophets of Islām.

Jesus in Islām is considered a beloved messenger of *Allāh.* He is not considered a God or a son of God, since *Allāh* is not a human being, nor does He have a wife or children. Jesus was born to no father, and he is not that different from Adam who was created from clay, and had no father or mother.

### 1.6.4 Angels and the Day of Judgment

Muslims believe that there are unseen creatures such as angels created by *Allāh* in the Universe for special missions. They do not bread nor are they at all the females that the unbelievers thought them to be.

Muslims believe that there is a Day of Judgment where all people of the world throughout the history of mankind till the last day of life on earth, will be brought for accounting, reward, and punishment.

### 1.6.5 Innocence of Man at Birth

Muslims believe that people are born free of sin. It is only after they reach the age of puberty and it is only after they commit sins that they are to be charged for their mistakes. No soul is responsible for the sins of other souls. Nevertheless, the door of forgiveness through true repentance is always open. So the idea of the original sin is rejected in Islām. The *Qur'ān* states that Adam and Eve *(Ḥawwā')* repented to *Allāh* after they disobeyed Him, and that *Allāh* accepted their repentance and forgave them.

### 1.6.6 Salvation

Islām teaches that people must work out their salvation through the guidance of *Allāh.* A Muslim has to combine his belief and practice in his daily life activities. Hence no one can act on behalf of someone else or even intercede between him and *Allāh.* At the same time *Allāh* does not accept lip service from people.

In Islām, there is no third party between people and *Allāh*, nor are there religious men or people like priests or pastors.

### 1.6.7 State and Religion

Muslims believe that Islām is a total and complete way of life. As such, the teachings of Islām do not separate religion from politics. As a matter of fact, state and religion are under the obedience of *Allāh* through the teachings of Islām. An Islāmic State is a state ruled by the Islāmic Law that is obtained from the *Qur'ān* and the *Sunnah*.

When people nowadays use the term Islāmic countries, they usually mean countries where Muslims are the vast majority. This does not mean that such a country is an Islāmic State, since many Islāmic countries are now ruled by non-Islāmic laws.

The principle of *Shūrā* is one of the necessary requirements for the state to be an Islāmic. It means that the leader of the state consults with the people concerning matters that are not defined in the *Qur'ān* or the *Sunnah*. However, it is important to mention that the principle of democracy defined as the majority ruling is not approved in Islām, since the ultimate ruling is for *Allāh*. Even a majority of 100% cannot, for example, allow drinking alcohol or make the prayers four instead of five. Discretion and reasoning apply to those matters that are not defined in the *Qur'ān* and the *Sunnah*.

## 1.7 Practices of Islām

*Allāh* instructed Muslims to practice what they believed in. In Islām there are five pillars, namely:

### 1.7.1 Creed (Shahādah)

The verbal commitment and pledge that there is no god but *Allāh* and that Muḥammad (s.a.w.) is the Messenger of *Allāh*, is considered to be the Creed of Islām.

### 1.7.2 Prayers (Ṣalāh)

The performance of five daily prayers is required of Muslims. These prayers have to be performed on specific times during the day and the night. These five obligatory prayers are: *Fajr* (Dawn), *Ẕuhr* (Noon), *'Aṣr* (Afternoon), *Maghrib* (Sunset), and *'Ishā'* (Late Night). Each prayer is called *Ṣalāh*.

The Friday congregational prayer *(Jumu'ah)* is also a must for Muslim men and optional for Muslim women. It has to be performed in the Mosque. It can also be performed in any convenient place when there is no Mosque in the area.

There are many optional prayers that Muslims perform along with those obligatory prayers.

A Muslim may pray anywhere in the world whether he/she is in a Mosque, a house, an office, or outside. The whole world is a place of worship. However, the reward is much greater when the prayers are performed in groups. Congregational prayers *(Jamā'ah)* in the Mosques are strongly recommended for Muslim men, while praying in the Mosques is optional for women.

Some special prayers also exist like praying before burying a dead Muslim, praying before travelling, praying on the *'Eid* days, and praying to get guidance when one cannot decide between two choices.

### 1.7.3 Fasting (Ṣawm)

Fasting is a total abstinence from food and liquids from dawn to sunset during the entire lunar month of *Ramadhān*. Married Muslims have also to refrain from intimate intercourse from dawn to sunset during that period. Muslims can still enjoy all these things during the night time of *Ramadhān* from sunset until dawn. They usually eat a meal right after sunset called *Ifṭār* which means breakfast and another light meal right before dawn called *Saḥūr*.

Recommended during this month is also a nightly prayer called *At-Tarāwīḥ* or *Al-Qiyām*. Most Muslims do this prayer in a group in the Mosque.

Muslims have more dinner invitations during the month of *Ramadhān* than they have during the year. The poor and the needy are among the first to be invited to such dinners.

### 1.7.4 Purifying Alms (Zakāh)

This is an annual payment of a certain percentage of a Muslim's property which is distributed among the poor or other rightful beneficiaries exclusively named in the *Qur'ān*. The property has to exceed a certain minimum to be subject to *Zakāh*, and has to have been owned for a lunar year. For example, it is 2.5% of the assets that exceed a certain minimum and have been owned for at least a lunar year.

### 1.7.5 Pilgrimage (Ḥajj)

The performance of pilgrimage to Makkah is required once in a lifetime, if means are available. Sacrifice of camels, cows, sheep, or goats, during *Ḥajj* is in memory of the trials and tribulations of Prophet Abraham, his wife Hagar, and his eldest son Prophet Ishmael. This sacrifice has nothing to do with the idea of sacrifice in some other religions where people believe that their sins are transferred to the sacrificed animal. Such an idea is rejected in Islām.

## 1.8 Other Related Aspects

### 1.8.1 Calendar

Islāmic practices are based on the lunar calendar. However Muslims also use the Gregorian calendar in their daily religious lives. Hence, the Islāmic calendar includes both the common era and the migration *(Hijrah)* year of Prophet Muḥammad (s.a.w.) from Makkah to Madīnah in the year of 623 C.E.

### 1.8.2 Celebrations ('Eids)

Muslims have two celebrations of *'Eids*: namely *'Eid* of Sacrifice *('Eid Al-Adhḥā)* and *'Eid* of Fast Breaking *('Eid Al-Fiṭr)*. The *'Eid* of Sacrifice is in remembrance of the sacrifice to be by Prophet Abraham of his son Ishmael. The *'Eid* of Breakfasting comes after the end of the fasting month of *Ramadhān*.

### 1.8.3 Diets

Islām allows Muslims to eat everything which is good for the health. It restricts certain items such as pork and its by-products, alcohol, and any narcotic or addictive drugs. Among the prohibited food is the meat of animals that are strangled, beaten to death, killed by a fall, killed by being smitten with the horn, and which beast have eaten, except those that have been slaughtered in the proper manner.

Among the forbidden food are the quadrupeds that seize their prey with their paws and teeth or talons, such as cats and tigers; and among the birds; crows, kites, eagles, and some other birds. Other prohibited food includes the flesh of elephants, the flesh of any animal dying a natural death, the blood, the flesh of those animals that on which any name other than the name of *Allāh* has been invoked when slaughtered, like those slaughtered for idols.

Prevention is better than treatment of a disease, and dieting is the safest way to better health. It is good to mention here that the personality, character, behavior, and overall performance of the individual, are affected by the food eaten, and therefore, one has to select the best type of food for his good health.

There is thus a linkage between physical and mental health. A proverb related to this subject has been narrated as saying: "A sound mind is in a sound body".

### 1.8.4 Place of Worship

The place of worship is called a Mosque or a *Masjid.* There are three holy places of worship for Muslims in the world. These are: *Al-Masjid Al-Ḥarām* in Makkah, *Al-Masjid An-Nabawī* in Madīnah, and *Al-Masjid Al-Aqṣā* adjacent to Dome of the Rock in Jerusalem.

A Muslim may pray anywhere in the world whether he/she is in a Mosque, a house, an office, or outside. The whole world is a place of worship. It is preferable that Muslims pray in a congregation, however, they may also pray individually anywhere.

### 1.8.5 Holiday

The holy day of the Muslims is Friday. It is a sacred day in the sight of *Allāh* for many reasons. Muslims join together shortly after noon on Friday for the Friday Congregational *(Jumu'ah)* prayer in a Mosque. Attending such a prayer in Mosques is a must for men while it is an option for women, who can pray at home instead.

The prayer leader *(Imām)* gives a sermon *(Khuṭbah)* and leads the Congregational Prayer.

The concept of the weekly holiday in Islām is different from that in other religions. Muslims can work on that day except during the time of the congregational prayer, when they are supposed to observe the prayer. Muslims do not believe that *Allāh* rested on any day, nor does He ever get tired.

## 1.9 Muslims

### 1.9.1 Distribution of Muslims

There are over one billion Muslims distributed in the world today. Muslims are 90% to 99% of the population in Muslim countries such as: Indonesia, Pakistan, Bangladesh, Turkey, Afghanistan, some African countries, and all of the Arab countries.

Muslims are also more than 55% in Malaysia. There are also great numbers of Muslims in other countries such as the European and African countries. There are for example over 50 million Muslims in the southern parts of what is now called the U.S.S.R., and over 100 million Muslims in India.

Muslims have also become the largest minority in North America and in some European countries like France. For example there are between five and eight million Muslims in North America. They are distributed in its major cities such as New York, Detroit, Boston, Toledo, Chicago, St. Louis, Los Angeles, San Francisco, Houston, Miami, Cedar Rapids (Iowa), London (Canada), Toronto, Montreal, Ottawa, Windsor, Winnipeg, Calgary, Edmonton, Vancouver, and many more.

### 1.9.2 Contributions of Muslims

Muslims of the early period of the Islāmic era were pioneers in medicine, chemistry, physics, navigation, arts, poetry, philosophy, mathematics, algebra, logarithms, calculus, astronomy, and social sciences. There are now 10,000 words in English whose roots are from the Arabic language. Arabic was the language of science and technology, and now it is one of the six major languages of the U.N.

Islāmic scientific genius introduced the Arabic numerals and the zero without which modern science could not have been developed. The sciences of Muslims were translated into Latin and passed on to the West. The scientific books of Muslims were used as texts in various European academic institutions up to the seventeenth century of the Common Era. Cities of world enlightenment were Cordova, Timbuktu, Seville, Fez, Tunis, Cairo, Damascus, Baghdad, Makkah, Madīnah, and others. The oldest academic universities in the world are *Al-Azhar* (Cairo), *Al-Qairawān* (Tunisia), and *Al-Qarawiyīn* (Morocco).

Muslims have already established community centers, organizations, schools, and places of worship in Europe and North America. They live in peace and harmony among themselves and among other groups of people in the society. The rate of crime among Muslims is very minimal. Muslims in North America and Europe are highly educated and have added to the success of scientific and technological fields. They have also added to the beauty of these societies and are trying to improve the status and the systems therein.

## 1.10 Non-Muslims

Muslims are required to be just to all people irrespective of their faith. They are also required to respect all those who are faithful and God-conscious people who received messages from *Allāh*. After all, the prophets of the Jews and the Christians are indeed the prophets of the Muslims. Prophet Muḥammad (s.a.w.) came to the Christians, the Jews, and the pagans as well as to all mankind. Christians and Jews are asked in return to respect Muslims. Christians and Jews are called "People of the Book" in the *Qur'ān*. Muslims are asked to call on the People of the Book for common terms, namely, to worship *Allāh*, and to work together to solve the problems of the society.

Christians and Jews have lived peacefully with Muslims for over fourteen centuries in the Middle East and in other Asian and African countries. Christians were welcomed by Prophet Muḥammad (s.a.w.) in Madīnah and a treaty of peace was signed. The second *Caliph 'Omar*, did not pray in the Church in Jerusalem so as not to give the Muslims an excuse to take it over. Christians entrusted the Muslims, and as such the key of the Church in Jerusalem is still in the hands of the Muslims. Jews fled from Spain during the Inquisition, and were welcomed by the Muslims. They settled in the heart of the Islāmic Caliphate. They enjoyed positions in the Islāmic State. Crusaders invaded the Middle East and occupied it for about 200 years. This occupation was accompanied with torture and persecution to the local people. However, when *Ṣalāḥ Ad-Dīn* liberated the land, he treated them with respect.

Throughout the Muslims world, churches, synagogues, and missionary schools were built within the Muslim neighborhoods.

Such places were protected by the Muslims even during the contemporary crises in the Muslim world. Non-Muslims have flourished in the Muslim world. The mere existence of their presence in large numbers in the Muslim world today proves the justice and tolerance of Islām and Muslims. Tolerance, justice, and coexistence are among the main teachings of Islām that lead to mutual understanding and a better way of life among all people. Islām does not allow Muslims to impose their belief on others. The *Qur'ān* states that {{*there is no compulsion in religion*}} *[Al-Qur'ān: Al-Baqarah (2:256)]*.

# Chapter 2

# ISLĀMIC GLOSSARIES

When Muslims speak to non-Muslims they usually use certain words and phrases that are understood mainly by Muslims in different parts of the world. These terms are taken from the *Qur'ān* and from the sayings of Prophet Muḥammad (s.a.w.). When Muslims write they use abbreviated words that are understood by Muslims only.

In either case whether the terms are used verbally or in the written form, they sound foreign to the non-Muslims. Therefore, it was believed that it would be for the benefit of the non-Muslims that these words, terms, abbreviations, and phrases be explained in a simple way so that they will be understood without difficulty. It is only through communication and mutual understanding that people can live in peace, harmony, concord, and happiness.

In this chapter, the authors wish to present a selected number of terms and glossaries that are used quite often. The following is a partial list with some descriptions:

## 2.1 Allāh

The true name for the Creator of the Universe is called *Allāh*. He is the Merciful, the Beneficent, the Knowledgeable, the Protector, the Mighty, the God, the Forgiver, the Provider, the Exalted, the Lord, the All-Knowing, the All-Hearing, the All-Seeing, the Magnificent, the Wise, the Loving, the First, the Last, and the Eternal.

The *Qur'ān* mentions 99 beautiful names for *Allāh* through which Muslims do recognize Him, appreciate His favors, and understand their duties toward Him, and His responsibilities for the whole Universe.

## 2.2 Muḥammad (s.a.w.)

The last and the final prophet and messenger of *Allāh* to mankind is called Muḥammad (s.a.w.). He was born in 570 C.E. at Makkah (Mecca), and at the age of forty he received the Message of Islām from *Allāh* through Angel Gabriel *(Jibrīl)*.

The Message of Islām was revealed to him in Makkah and Madīnah in Arabia. He died at the age of 63 (lunar years) and his grave is in his house, which happened to be in his *Masjid* in Madīnah *(Al-Masjid An-Nabawī)*.

Muḥammad (s.a.w.) lived as an honest man, and he practiced the teachings exactly the same way he preached. He was a prophet, a messenger, a husband, a father, a religious leader, a political leader, and a reformer. He is the summation, the culmination, and the purification for all the previous prophets that came before him. He is the most influential man in the history of mankind.

## 2.3 Islām

Islām is an Arabic word the root of which is *Silm* and *Salām*. It means among others: peace, greeting, salutation, obedience, loyalty, allegiance, and submission to the will of the Creator of the Universe.

Islām is the last and final religion to all mankind and to all generations irrespective of color, race, nationality, ethnic background, language, or social position.

The religion of Islām is not to be confused with Mohammedanism. The latter is a misnomer to Islām. Muslims do not accept this name as it gives wrong information about Islām and Muslims.

## 2.4 Muslim(s)

Any person who believes in the creed and the teachings of Islām is called a Muslim. More than one billion Muslims are found in different parts of the world. They are not to be confused with Arabs, as the latter may include Christians, agnostics, or other non-Muslims.

Muslims in America are between five and eight million and they are living in peace and harmony with their non-Muslim friends and neighbors. They are highly educated and are trying to contribute to and to improve the status of the society they live in, technically and socially.

The word Mohammedans is a misnomer to the believers in Islām. Muslims do not accept this nickname as it gives a wrong and a bad connotation about them. The followers are called Muslims, i.e., those who believe in *Allāh* and submit to His Will.

The word Muslim in some places in the *Qur'ān* is also used to refer to all the ones who believed in *Allāh* and His messages and submitted to Him, even before Muḥammad (s.a.w.). Many prophets, like *Nūḥ* (Noah), *Ibrāhīm* (Abraham), *Mūsā* (Moses), and *'Īsā* (Jesus), are called Muslims in the *Qur'ān*.

## 2.5 Qur'ān

The holy book of Islām is called the *Qur'ān*. It was revealed unto Muḥammad (s.a.w.) from *Allāh* through Angel Gabriel *(Jibrīl)* for a period of 23 years. There is only one *Qur'ān* in the whole world and it is in Arabic language. The *Qur'ān* has one text, one language, and one dialect. It has been memorized by millions of Muslims in different parts of the world.

The *Qur'ān* is composed of 114 *Sūrah* (chapters). It is to be read and recited with rules and regulations. When to be touched and to be recited, a Muslim is to be in a state of cleanliness and purity.

The authenticity and the totality of the *Qur'ān* have been documented and recognized. The *Qur'ān* can not be translated at all as the *Qur'ān* is the exact words of *Allāh*. Any translation is considered to be the explanation to the meaning of the *Qur'ān*.

The *Qur'ān* is so rich and comprehensive in matter that it can easily guide men and women in all walks of their life. It is the ultimate source of guidance for people in all aspects of their spiritual and material lives.

The names and attributes that are given to the *Qur'ān* in the *Qur'ān* speak for themselves. The *Qur'ān* is described to be the recited, distinction between good and evil, reminder, admonition, judgment, wisdom, guidance, revelation, mercy, spirit, goodness, explainer, *Allāh's* favor, maintainer, guardian, light, truth, and covenant of *Allāh*.

The *Qur'ān* is also described to be bounteous, glorious, mighty, honored, exalted, purified, wonderful, blessed, and confirming the truth of previous revelations. The *Qur'ān* has practically proved the truth and effectiveness of all of its names and epithets in the life of all true believers, who practiced its teachings sincerely and devoutly.

The *Qur'ān* has a universal appeal, regardless of people's color, creed, nationality, and geographical divisions of the world. The goal of life, as addressed in the *Qur'ān*, is to live according to what *Allāh* created us for, which is to worship *Allāh*, and to obey His commandments in this life, which are of course, in the interest of people, and to gain going to Heaven and escape going to Hell in the hereafter. The real success is going to Heaven and the real failure is going to Hell, as the *Qur'ān* states.

Those who are entirely lost in their material gains and luxury, without cultivating their spiritual and moral qualities, are declared by *Allāh* (s.w.t.) to be like animals, rather worse than them. The ones who do not believe in *Allāh* or follow His commandments are also described in many places of the *Qur'ān* to be dead, deaf, mute, and blind. The real living, hearing, speaking, and seeing are caused by the true belief in the heart. So our need for learning, studying, and following the *Qur'ān* should come before our need for breathing, drinking, and eating to survive, because life without such guidance is a miserable life that leads to eternal punishment.

## 2.6 Ḥadīth

The sayings and the traditions of Prophet Muḥammad (s.a.w.) are called the *Ḥadīth.* These are the real explanation, interpretation, and the living example of the Prophet (s.a.w.) for the teachings of the *Qur'ān.* His sayings are found in books called the *Ḥadīth* books.

The six famous collectors of *Ḥadīth* are *Imām Al-Bukhārī, Imām Muslim, Imām An-Nasā'ī, Imām Abū Dāwood, Imām At-Tirmiẓī,* and *Imām Ibn Mājah.*

## 2.7 Sunnah

In general, the word *Sunnah* means habit, practice, customary procedure, or action, norm and usage sanctioned by tradition. In specific, any time the word *Sunnah* is mentioned, it is to refer to Prophet Muḥammad (s.a.w.). Here it means his sayings, practices, and living habits. The *Ḥadīth* of the Prophet (s.a.w.) is part of his *Sunnah.*

The two major legal sources of jurisprudence in Islām are the *Qur'ān* and the *Sunnah.*

The *Sunnah* may confirm what is mentioned in the *Qur'ān,* interpret and explain it, specify what is meant by some general verses, limit and restrict the meaning of some verses in it, or may explain something that has not been revealed in the *Qur'ān.*

The *Sunnah* has a high authority in Islām; and *Allāh* in many places in the *Qur'ān* orders the Muslims to follow the teachings of Prophet Muḥammad (s.a.w.).

## 2.8 Sīrah

The writings of the companions of the Prophet (s.a.w.) about him, his personality, his life history, and his ways of handling different situations is called *Sīrah*. The famous collections of the *Sīrah* are *Aṭ-Ṭabarī*, *Ibn Isḥāq*, and *Ibn Hishām*.

The *Sīrah* is a source of reference that Muslims rely on in their daily life situations and problems.

## 2.9 Fiqh

The meaning of the word *Fiqh* is understanding, comprehension, knowledge, and jurisprudence in Islām. A jurist is called a *Faqīh* who is an expert in matters of Islāmic legal matters.

A *Faqīh* is to pass verdicts within the rules of the Islāmic Law namely the *Sharī'ah*.

The most famous scholars of *Fiqh* in the history of Muslims are the founders of the four schools of thought in Islām: *Imām Mālik, Imām Ash-Shāfi'ī, Imām Abū Ḥanīfah*, and *Imām Aḥmad.*

Any thing or action in Islām falls within the following five categories of *Fiqh*:

1. **Fardh (Must):** This category is a must for the Muslim to do such as the five daily prayers. Doing the *Fardh* counts as a good deed, and not doing it is considered a bad deed or a sin.

   It is also called *Wājib* except for *Imām Abū Ḥanīfah*, who makes the *Wājib* a separate category between the *Fardh* and the *Mubāḥ*.

2. **Mandūb (Recommended):** This category is recommended for the Muslim to do such as the extra prayers after *Ẓuhr* and *Maghrib*. Doing the *Mandūb* counts as a good deed, and not doing it does not count as a bad deed or a sin.

3. **Mubāḥ (Allowed):** This category is left undecided and is left for the person, such as eating apples or oranges. Doing or not doing the *Mubāḥ* does not count as a good or bad deed.

   The intention of the person can change the ***Mubāh*** to ***Fardh***, *Mandūb*, *Makrūh*, or *Ḥarām*.

   Other things could also change the status of ***Mubāh***. For example, any *Mubāh* becomes *Ḥarām* if it is proven harmful, and any necessary thing to fulfill a ***Fardh*** is a ***Fardh*** too.

4. **Makrūh (Hated):** This category is a detested and hated such as growing fingernails or sleeping on the stomach. Not doing the *Makrūh* counts as a good deed and doing it does not count as a bad deed.

5. **Ḥarām (Prohibited):** This category is prohibited for the Muslim to do such as lying and stealing. Doing the *Ḥarām* counts as a bad deed, and not doing it counts as a good deed.

   *Imām Abū Ḥanīfah* also puts another category between the *Makrūh* and the *Ḥarām*. It is called ***Karāhah Taḥrīmiyyah*** which means hated almost to the level of Ḥarām.

## 2.10 Sharī'ah

The root of this word is *Shara'a*; and some other names of it are *Shar'*, *Shir'ah* and *Tashrī'*. The *Sharī'ah* is the revealed and the canonical laws of the religion of Islām.

The legislative power in the government lies in the hands of the legislative assembly. The legislators are to make rules and regulations within the scope and dimensions of the *Qur'ān* and the *Sunnah* of the Prophet (s.a.w.). These rules constitute the *Sharī'ah*.

## 2.11 Nabī

The meaning of the word *Nabī* is a prophet. To be a prophet he should receive a revelation from *Allāh* that doesn't necessarily mean a revealed book. When a prophet is instructed to deliver his message to a certain group of people, he is a messenger. Therefore, every messenger is a prophet but not every prophet is a messenger. It is stated in the *Qur'ān* that there are no more prophets and messengers after Muḥammad.

## 2.12 Rasūl

The meaning of the word *Rasūl* is a messenger. *Allāh* sent many prophets and messengers to mankind. Amongst them, the names of twenty-five are mentioned in the *Qur'ān.* From within the list, the *Qur'ān* states the names of five *Rusul* who are the Mighty ones. These are: *Nūḥ* (Noah), *Ibrāhīm* (Abraham), *Mūsā* (Moses), *'Īsā* (Jesus), and Muḥammad (s.a.w.).

## 2.13 Khalīfah

The word *Khalīfah* or Caliph is a person who is a vice gerent of someone else. Man is considered to be the Caliph of Almighty *Allāh* on earth. He is to represent Him and execute His wishes. The title *Amīr Al-Mu'minīn* is also used to refer to the Caliph, which means the leader of the believers.

Those persons who succeeded Prophet Muḥammad (s.a.w.) were called Caliphs. They were selected and appointed to assume the responsibility of leadership of the Muslims.

The immediate Caliphs were *Abū Bakr Aṣ-Ṣiddīq, 'Omar Ibn Al-Khaṭṭāb, 'Othmān Ibn 'Affān,* and *'Alī Ibn Abī Ṭālib.* These were given the nickname of *Al-Khulafā' Ar-Rāshidūn* (The Guided Caliphs).

## 2.14 Imām

*Imām* is a religious leader. Any person who leads a congregational prayer is called an *Imām.* A religious leader who also leads his community in the political affairs may be called an *Imām*, an *Amīr*, or a Caliph. However, an *Imām* is not infallible. He is responsible for his mistakes to all the members of the community and above all he is responsible to Almighty *Allāh.*

## 2.15 Shaikh

The word *Shaikh* is a title or a nickname for an elderly person or a religious leader in a community. This title is also given to a wise person.

The meaning of the word *Shaikh* has been distorted, misused, and abused by some mass media to reflect wrong meanings.

## 2.16 Ṣalāh

*Ṣalāh* is an Arabic word to mean a spiritual relationship and communication between the creature and his Creator. *Ṣalāh* is one of the five pillars of Islām. A special communication *(Ṣalāh)* is to take place five times a day for a Muslim: *Fajr* (Dawn), *Zuhr* (Noon), *'Aṣr* (Afternoon), *Maghrib* (Sunset), and *'Ishā'* (Late Night).

*Ṣalāh* is to be performed with mental concentration, verbal communication, vocal recitation, and physical movement to attain the spiritual uplift, peace, harmony, and concord. There is a congregational prayer on Friday noon *(Ṣalātul Jumu'ah)* with a sermon *(Khuṭbah)* to be delivered by a religious leader *(Imām)* called *Khaṭīb.*

To perform *Ṣalāh*, a Muslim has to have ablution *(Wudhū').* He/she should make sure that cleanliness of body, clothing, and place are attained before performing *Ṣalāh.*

*Ṣalāh* is not to be confused with prayer; the latter could be interpreted as supplication *(Du'ā')*.

## 2.17 Ṣawm

*Ṣawm* or *Ṣiyām* is to mean total abstinence of food and liquid from dawn to sunset for one whole lunar month. For those who are married, they are to abstain from sexual relations during that time too.

*Ṣawm* (Fasting) takes place during the ninth month of the lunar calendar called *Ramadhān*. *Ṣawm* is one of the five pillars of Islām.

Total fasting is also a training process to attain self-restraint, self-control, self-discipline, self-obedience, self-education, and self-evaluation.

Few people are excused from fasting during *Ramadhān*. Some are required to make up later for the days they didn't fast such as the travellers (over 50 miles by any means), sick, pregnant women, women nursing babies, and women during their periods. Other excused people are required to feed a poor person one meal per each day they do not fast if they can afford it, such as the elderly people and the ones who have permanent diseases like ulcers.

## 2.18 Zakāh

One of the five pillars of Islām is *Zakāh*, which means purification and increment of one's wealth.

A Muslim who has money beyond a certain quantity is to pay the *Zakāh*. It is also called the alms due or poor due. It is to be used in eight categories for welfare of the society that are mentioned in the *Qur'ān*, namely: the poor, the needy, the sympathizers, the captives, the debtors, the cause of *Allāh*, the wayfarers, and for those who are to collect it.

The amount to be collected is 2.5%, 5%, or 10%, depending on the assets and the method used to produce it. For example, it is 2.5% of the assets that have been owned over a year, 5% of the wheat when irrigated by the farmer, and 10% of the wheat that is irrigated by rain.

## 2.19 Ḥajj

*Ḥajj* is an Arabic word which means the performance of pilgrimage to Makkah in Arabia. It is one of the five pillars of Islām. A Muslim is to perform *Ḥajj* at least once in his/her life, if means and health allow.

There are rules and regulations and specific dress to be followed. It is to take place during the last month of the lunar calendar called the month of *Ẓul-Ḥijjah.*

## 2.20 Jihād

It is an Arabic word the root of which is *Jāhada*, which means to strive for a better way of life. The nouns are *Juhd, Mujāhid, Jihād,* and *Ijtihād*. The other meanings are: endeavor, strain, exertion, effort, diligence, fighting to defend one's life, land, and religion.

*Jihād* should not be confused with Holy War; the latter does not exist in Islām nor will Islām allow its followers to be involved in a Holy War. The latter refers to the Holy War of the Crusaders.

*Jihād* is not a war to force the faith on others, as many people think of it. It should never be interpreted as a way of compulsion of the belief on others, since there is an explicit verse in the *Qur'ān* that says: {{*There is no compulsion in religion*}} *[Al-Qur'ān: Al-Baqarah (2:256)].*

*Jihād* is not also a defensive war only, but a war against any unjust regime. If such a regime exists, a war is to be waged against the leaders, but not against the people of that country. People should be freed from the unjust regimes and influences so that they can freely choose to believe in *Allāh.*

Not only in peace but also in war Islām prohibits terrorism, kidnapping, and hijacking, when carried against civilians. Whoever commits such violations is considered a murderer in Islām, and is to be punished by the Islāmic State. During wars, Islām prohibits Muslim soldiers from harming civilians, women, children, elderly, and the religious men like priests and rabbis. It also prohibits cutting down trees and destroying civilian constructions.

## 2.21 Ḥalāl/Ḥarām

These are two Arabic words to mean lawful and unlawful. The standards are based on the ***Qur'ān*** and the ***Ḥadīth***; and Muslims are to abide in their daily life activities by the teachings of their standards.

These two concepts are very important when one talks about moral, physical, spiritual, medical, biological, and dietetic aspects of Islām. Muslims talk regularly about ***Ḥalāl*** and ***Ḥarām*** for anything they do.

When Muslims talk about meat, for example, they use the terminology of ***Ẓabīḥah*** to mean ***Ḥalāl***; hence it will be lawful to be eaten.

## 2.22 'Eid

The word ***'Eid*** is an Arabic name to mean a festivity, a celebration, a recurring happiness, and a feast. In Islām, there are two major ***'Eids*** namely the Feast of ***Ramadhān ('Eid Al-Fiṭr)*** and the Feast of Sacrifice ***('Eid Al-Adhḥā)***. The first ***'Eid*** is celebrated by Muslims after fasting the month of ***Ramadhān*** as a matter of thanks and gratitude to Almighty ***Allāh***. It takes place on the first day of ***Shawwāl***, the tenth month of the lunar calendar. The second ***'Eid*** is the Feast of Sacrifice and it is to be celebrated for the memory of Prophet ***Ibrāhīm*** trying to sacrifice his son ***Ismā'īl*** (Ishmael). This ***'Eid*** lasts four days between the

$10^{th}$ and the $13^{th}$ day of *Ẓul-Ḥijjah*, the twelfth month of the lunar calendar.

## 2.23 Festivities

Other than the two general feasts, there are few festivities that Muslims do enjoy. These are related to different activities or functions. Some of these festivities are:

- **'Aqīqah:** It is a dinner reception to be made after a child is born. Relatives, friends, and neighbors are invited for such an occasion.
- **Walīmah:** It is a dinner reception to be made after a marriage is consummated. It is offered by the parents and/or by the newly married couples. Friends, relatives, and neighbors are also invited.

## 2.24 Lunar Calendar

In their religious duties, Muslims depend on solar and lunar calendars. The latter is shorter than the solar by twelve days. Fasting the month of *Ramadhān*, celebrating the two major feasts (*'Eid Al-Fiṭr* and *'Eid Al-Adhḥā*), performing the pilgrimage to Makkah, and other religious activities depend upon the lunar months.

The names of the lunar months are: *Muḥarram*, *Ṣafar*, *Rabī' Al-Awwal*, *Rabī' Al-Ākhar*, *Jamādā Al-'Ūlā*, *Jamādā Al-Ākhirah*, *Rajab*, *Sha'bān*, *Ramadhān*, *Shawwāl*, *Ẓul-Qi'dah*, and *Ẓul-Ḥijjah*.

The timing of the five daily prayers depends on solar system.

## 2.25 Masjid

The place of worship for the Muslims is called in Arabic a *Masjid*; the plural of which is called *Masājid*. The English meaning is a

Mosque. Muslims can pray to Allāh anywhere; however, they are demanded to establish mosques in their neighborhood. The mosques are for the five daily prayers, for the weekly Friday prayer, and for other social, cultural, educational, and religious purposes.

There are three holy Mosques in the world that Muslims are asked to visit and to pray in. These are *Al-Masjid Al-Ḥarām* in Makkah, *Al-Masjid An-Nabawī* in Madīnah (both are in Arabia), and *Al-Masjid Al-Aqṣā* in Jerusalem (Palestine). The first one has *Al-Ka'bah*, and the second one is the Mosque of the Prophet.

The third one was the former *Qiblah* of Muslims, and the sight to where *Allāh* took Prophet Muḥammad (s.a.w.) by night from the Sacred Mosque in Makkah. Muḥammad (s.a.w.) was then raised to Heaven from that place and brought back to Makkah, all in one night. The Dome of the Rock, in Jerusalem, was built a few decades after the death of Prophet Muḥammad (s.a.w.).

## 2.26 Aẓān

The call for the daily prayers is called *Aẓān.* The person who calls the *Aẓān* is called a *Mu'aẓẓin.* A *Mu'aẓẓin* calls the *Aẓān* five times a day before Muslims are to perform their daily *Ṣalāh* (Prayer).

The *Aẓān* is composed of specific words and phrases to be recited loudly in the Arabic language so that the neighbors can recognize the time schedule for the prayers.

## 2.27 Iqāmah

*Iqāmah* is an Arabic word that refers to the second call for the prayer which follows the first call *(Aẓān). Iqāmah* means that the prayer is ready to start. It is to be recited in Arabic before every obligatory prayer. It is composed of specific words and phrases very closely related to the *Aẓān.*

## 2.28 Rukū‘

The root of this word is *Raka‘a* which means bow down. During prayers *(Ṣalāh)*, a Muslim is to make *Rukū‘* (bowing down) in respect to *Allāh.*

While in a position of *Rukū‘* a Muslim is to glorify *Allāh* three times.

## 2.29 Sujūd

The root of this word is *Sajada* which means that a person makes prostration to *Allāh* in his daily prayers. While in the position of *Sujūd*, a Muslim is to praise Almighty *Allāh* and to glorify Him.

During the position of *Sujūd*, a Muslim is to make sure that his/her forehead, nose, hands, knees, and toes, are all touching the floor.

## 2.30 Sūrah

The *Qur'ān* is composed of 114 chapters, each of which is called a *Sūrah.* The plural of *Sūrah* is called *Suwar*, which means chapters.

## 2.31 Āyah

The Arabic meaning of *Āyah* is a miracle and a sign. The *Qur'ān* is considered to be a miracle in itself. Each verse or sentence is called an *Āyah* or a miracle. The plural of *Āyah* is called *Āyāt*, which means miracles.

## 2.32 Ḥifẕ

The Arabic root of this word is *Ḥafiẕa* which means to memorize. In the religious sense, Muslims try to memorize the whole *Qur'ān.* Any person who achieves this task is called a *Ḥāfiẕ.*

A *Ḥāfiẕ* is recognized by his community and is given certain privileges. There are millions of Muslims who make *Ḥifẕ* of the whole *Qur'ān*.

## 2.33 s.a.w.

These letters are abbreviations for the words *"Ṣallā Allāhu 'Alaihi Wa Sallam"*, which means: may the blessings and the peace of *Allāh* be upon him.

When the name of Prophet Muḥammad is mentioned, a Muslim is to respect him and to invoke this statement of peace upon him.

## 2.34 p.b.u.h.

These letters are abbreviations for the words *Peace Be Upon Him* which are the meaning of the Arabic expression *" 'Alaihis Salām"*, which is an expression that is said when the name of a prophet is mentioned.

This expression is widely used by the English speaking Muslims. It is to be noticed here that this expression does not give the full meaning of *"Sallā Allāhu 'Alaihi Wa Sallam"*. Therefore, it is recommended that people do not use (p.b.u.h.) after the name of Prophet Muḥammad (s.a.w.); they should use *"Ṣallā Allāhu 'Alaihi Wa Sallam"* instead, or they may use the abbreviated form of (s.a.w.) in writing.

## 2.35 s.w.t.

These letters are abbreviations for the words of *"Subḥānahu Wa Ta'ālā"*. When the name of Almighty *Allāh* is pronounced, a Muslim is to show his respect to Him. The meaning of this statement is that *Allāh* is purified of having partners or a son.

## 2.36 Malā'ikah

These are the angels of *Allāh*. They are strict followers of the commands of *Allāh*. They have specific jobs to do, and they do not commit any sins at all. They are not at all the females that some of the unbelievers thought them to be. They were created by *Allāh* from light.

## 2.37 Jinn

These are spiritual beings that inhibit the world and are required to follow the orders of *Allāh* and are accountable for their deeds. They can be good or bad, just like people. The word *Jinn* in Arabic means hidden, which indicates that they are invisible creatures. They were created by *Allāh* from fire.

## 2.38 Shaiṭān

*Shaiṭān* (Satan) is the source of evil in the world. The plural name is *Shayāṭīn*. He always tries to misguide and mislead people. The *Qur'ān* states that Satan is not an angel but a member of the *Jinn*. His other name is *Iblīs*.

When *Allāh* created Adam, He ordered the angels as well as *Iblīs* to prostrate for Adam. They all obeyed that order of *Allāh* except *Iblīs*. His argument was that *Allāh* created Adam from clay and *Iblīs* from the flame of fire. Accordingly, *Iblīs* thought that he was better than Adam. Hence, *Allāh* told him that he will dwell in Hell. *Iblīs* asked *Allāh* for a postponement until the hereafter. *Allāh* granted his request. *Iblīs* swore that he would mislead and misguide all the people except those sincere and devoted worshipers of *Allāh*. *Allāh* told him that only the misguided ones would follow him and that He would fill Hell with him and his followers.

## 2.39 Sin Al-Bulūgh

This is the age of maturity or puberty. It is the age at which the Muslim is considered an adult and becomes accountable for his/her duties in Islām. There is no fixed age for that in terms of years and it is decided by three signs: having a menstruation period or pregnancy for girls, and being physically mature or having a wet dream for boys, growing pubic hair, or reaching the age of fifteen, whichever comes first.

## 2.40 Sin At-Tamyīz

This is the age of distinguishing. This age is used in *Fiqh* to decide the age before which the mother has the right to keep the child after divorce. It varies from one person to another. The age is reached when the child can take care of himself or herself and no longer needs an adult to help him/her eat, get dressed, and clean himself or herself. In the school of thought of *Abū Ḥanīfah*, it is seven years for the boy and nine years for the girl. The girl is given a longer time so that she can learn more of the habits of women.

## 2.41 Maḥram

A *Maḥram* is a man that a woman can never marry like a brother or a father. A brother-in-law is not considered a *Maḥram* in Islām since he can marry her after the death or divorce of his wife (her sister). A man can also marry his sister-in-law after the death of his brother (her husband) or after they get divorced. If a man and a woman get divorced because one of them accused the other with adultery in the court, without proving it *(Li'ān)*, the man is not considered a *Maḥram* for her, although he can never marry her again, according to the Islāmic law.

# Chapter 3

# ISLĀMIC EXPRESSIONS

Muslims throughout the world have learned from childhood to use certain expressions in their daily lives. These expressions are taken either from the *Qur'ān* and/or from the *Sunnah*. Muslims do use these phrases irrespective of their nationality, ethnic background, or language.

It is strange enough that an Arab Muslim going out from Makkah in Arabia to anywhere in the world, will find himself at home with the other Muslims. The same religious expressions, the same phrases, and the same sentences are used without difficulty to understand one another.

These expressions are used in writing as well as in verbal communication. These phrases have made the Muslims appreciate their religious values and teachings. Muslims find it easy to use such expressions since many of them cannot be translated easily without finding a series of sentences to explain them.

Non-Muslims who associate themselves with Muslims find it difficult to understand these phrases, sentences, and expressions. Many times the general understanding of the talk is lost due to the lack of knowledge for the meaning of such expressions.

This chapter is meant to explain some of the major

expressions in a simple language where non-Muslims will communicate with Muslims with better understanding. It is only through communication with the proper words, sentences, phrases, expressions, and paragraphs that people may realize how friendly and respectful they are to one another. The following is a partial list of these expressions:

## 3.1 A'ūẓu Billāhi Minashaiṭānir Rajīm

This is an expression and a statement that Muslims have to recite before reading the *Qur'ān*, before speaking, before doing any work, before making a supplication, before taking ablution, before entering the wash room, and before doing many other daily activities. The meaning of this phrase is: *"I seek refuge in Allāh from the outcast Satan"*. *Allāh* is the Arabic name of God.

Satan *(Shaiṭān)* is the source of evil and he always tries to misguide and mislead people. The *Qur'ān* states that Satan is not an angel but a member of the *Jinn*, which are spiritual beings created by *Allāh*. So the belief that Satan is a fallen angel is rejected in Islām.

## 3.2 Bismillāhir Raḥmānir Raḥīm

This is a phrase from the *Qur'ān* that is recited before reading the *Qur'ān*. It is to be read immediately after one reads the phrase: *"A'ūẓu Billāhi Minash-Shaiṭānir Rajīm"*.

This phrase is also recited before doing any activity. The meaning of it is: *"In the name of Allāh, the Most Beneficent, the Most Merciful"*.

## 3.3 Al-Ḥamdu Lillāhi Rabbil 'Ālamīn

This is a verse from the *Qur'ān* that Muslims recite and say many times per day. Other than being recited daily during prayers, a

Muslim reads this expression in every activity of his daily life. The meaning of it is *"Praise be to Allāh, the Lord of the worlds"*.

A Muslim invokes the praises of *Allāh* before he does his daily work; and when he finishes, he thanks *Allāh* for His favors. A Muslim is grateful to *Allāh* for all His blessings. It is a statement of thanks, appreciation, and gratitude from the creature to his Creator.

## 3.4 Lā Ilāha Illallāh

This expression is the most important one in Islām. It is the creed that every person has to say to be considered a Muslim. It is part of the first pillar of Islām. The meaning of which is: *"There is no lord worthy of worship except Allāh"*.

The second part of this first pillar is to say: *"Muḥammadun Rasūl Allāh"*, which means: *"Muḥammad is the Messenger of Allāh"*.

## 3.5 Muḥammadun Rasūlullāh

This statement is the second part of the first pillar of Islām. Its meaning is: *"Muḥammad is the Messenger of Allāh"*.

The other part of the first pillar is: *"There is no lord but Allāh"*.

The meaning of the second part is that Prophet Muḥammad is the last and final prophet and messenger of *Allāh* to mankind. He is the culmination, summation, and purification of the previous prophets of *Allāh* to humanity.

A Muslim says this statement many times everyday.

## 3.6 Allāhu Akbar

This statement is said by Muslims numerous times. During the call for prayer, during prayer, when they are happy, and wish to express their approval of what they hear, when they slaughter an animal, and when they want to praise a speaker, Muslims do say this expression of *Allāhu Akbar*. Actually, it is the most said expression in the world. Its meaning: *"Allāh is the Greatest"*. Muslims praise *Allāh* in every aspect of life; and as such they say *Allāhu Akbar*.

## 3.7 Subḥānahu Wa Ta'ālā

This is an expression that Muslims use whenever the name of *Allāh* is pronounced or written.

The meaning of this expression is: *"Allāh is pure of having partners and He is exalted from having a son"*.

Muslims believe that *Allāh* is the only God, the Creator of the Universe. He does not have partners or children.

Sometimes, Muslims use some other expressions when the name of *Allāh* is written or pronounced. Some of which are:

*" 'Azza Wa Jall"*: He is the Mighty and the Majestic.

*"Jalla Jalāluh"*: He is the Exalted Majestic.

## 3.8 Ṣadaqallāhul 'Aẕīm

This is a statement of truth that a Muslim says after reading any amount of verses from the *Qur'ān*. The meaning of it is: *"Allāh says the truth"*.

The *Qur'ān* is the exact words of *Allāh* in verbatim. When *Allāh* speaks, He says the truth; and when the *Qur'ān* is being recited, a Muslim is reciting the words of truth of *Allāh*. Hence, he says: *"Ṣadaqa Allāh Al-'Aẕim"*.

## 3.9 Ṣallallāhu 'Alaihi Wa Sallam

This is an expression that Muslims use whenever the name of Prophet Muḥammad (s.a.w.) is mentioned or written. The meaning of it is: *"May the blessings and the peace of Allāh be upon Him (Muḥammad)"*.

Another expression that is alternatively used is:

*"Alaihissalatu Wassalam"*. This expression means: *"On him (Muhammad) are the blessing and the peace (of Allah)"*.

*Allah* has ordered Muslims, in the *Qur'an,* to say such an expression. Muslims are informed that if they proclaim such a statement once. *Allah* will reward them ten times.

## 3.10 Radhiallāhu 'Anhu

This is an expression to be used by Muslims whenever a name of a companion of the Prophet (s.a.w.) is mentioned or used in writing. The meaning of this statement is: *"May Allāh be pleased with him"*.

Muslims are taught to be respectful to the elderly, to the leaders, and to those who contributed to the spread and success of Islām. They are to be grateful to the companions of the Prophet (s.a.w.) for their sacrifices, their leadership, and their contributions. Muslims are advised to use this phrase when such names are mentioned or written.

## 3.11 Assalāmu 'Alaikum

This is an expression that Muslims say whenever they meet one another. It is a statement of greeting with peace. The meaning of it is: *"Peace be upon you"*.

Muslims try to establish peace on earth even through the friendly relation of greeting and meeting one another.

The other forms are: *"Assalāmu 'Alaikum Wa Raḥmatullāh"*, which means: *"May the peace and the mercy of Allāh be upon you"*, and *"Assalāmu 'Alaikum Wa Raḥmatullāhi Wa Barakātuh"*, which means: *"May the peace, the mercy, and the blessings of Allāh be upon you"*.

## 3.12 Wa 'Alaikumus Salām

This is an expression that a Muslims is to say as an answer for the greeting. When a person greets another with a salutation of peace, the answer for the greeting is an answer of peace. The meaning of this statement is: *"And upon you is the peace"*. The other expressions are: *"Wa 'Alaikums Salām Wa Raḥmatullāh"*. and *"Wa 'Alaikums Salām Wa Raḥmatullāhi Wa Barakātuh"*.

## 3.13 Jazākallāhu Khayran

This is a statement of thanks and appreciation to be said to the person who does a favor. Instead of saying "thanks" *(Shukran)*, the Islāmic statement of thanks is to say this phrase. Its meaning is: *"May Allāh reward you for the good"*.

It is understood that human beings can't repay one another enough. Hence, it is better to request Almighty *Allāh* to reward the person who did a favor and to give him the best.

## 3.14 In Shā' Allāh

When a person wishes to plan for the future, when he promises, when he makes resolutions, and when he makes a pledge, he makes them with the permission and the will of *Allāh*. For this reason, a Muslim uses the *Qur'ānic* instructions by saying *"In Shā' Allāh"*. The meaning of this statement is: *"If Allāh wills"*.

Muslims are to strive hard and to put their trusts with *Allāh*. They leave the results in the hands of *Allāh*.

## 3.15 Mā Shā' Allāh

This is an expression that Muslims say whenever they are excited and surprised. When they wish to express their happiness, they use such an expression. The meaning of *"Mā Shā' Allāh"* is: *"Whatever Allāh wants"*, or: *"Whatever Allāh wants to give, He gives"*. This means that whenever *Allāh* gives something good to someone, blesses him, honors him, and opens the door of success in business, a Muslim says this statement of *"Mā Shā' Allāh"*.

It has become a tradition that whenever a person constructs a building, a house, or an office, he puts a plaque on the wall or the entrance with this statement. It is a sign of thanks and appreciation from the person to Almighty *Allāh* for whatever he was blessed with.

### 3. 16 Inna Lillahi Wa Inna Ilaihi Raji'un

When a Muslim is struck with a calamity, when he loses one of his loved ones, or when he has gone bankrupt, he should be patient and say this statement, the meaning of which is: *"We are from Allah and to Him we are returning"*.

Muslims believe that *Allah* is the One who gives and it is He who takes away. He is testing us. Hence, a Muslim submits himself to *Allah*. He is greatful and thankful to *Allah* for whatever he gets. On the other hand, he is patient and says this expression in times of turmoil and calamity.

## 3.17 Lā Ḥawla Wa Lā Q̲uwwata Illā Billāh

The meaning of this expression is: *"There is no power and no strength save in Allāh"*.

This expression is read by a Muslim when he is struck by a calamity, or is taken over by a situation beyond his control. A Muslim puts his trusts in the hands of *Allāh*, and submits himself to *Allāh*.

## 3.18 Astag̲h̲firullāh

This is an expression used by a Muslim when he wants to ask *Allāh* forgiveness. The meaning of it is: *"I ask Allāh forgiveness"*.

A Muslim says this phrase many times, even when he is talking to another person. When a Muslim abstains from doing wrong, or even when he wants to prove that he is innocent of an incident, he uses this expression of *"Astaghfirullāh"*. After every *Ṣalāh* (prayer), a Muslim says this statement three times.

## 3.19 Bārakallāh

This is an expression which means: *"May the blessings of Allāh (be upon you)"*.

When a Muslim wants to thank another person, he uses different statements to express his thanks, appreciation, and gratitude. One of them is to say *"Bāraka Allāh"*.

# Appendix A

# Further Reading

**For further reading about Islām in English, the following material is recommended:**

1. ***"The Holy Qur'ān"*, Arabic text, translation of the meanings, and commentary, 'Abdullāh Yūsuf 'Alī, American Trust Publications, 10900 W. Washington Street, Indianapolis, IN 46231, U.S.A., 1979.**
2. ***"The Holy Qur'ān"*, Arabic text and translation of the meanings, Muḥammad Marmaduke Pickthall, Muslim World League-Rabita, United Nations Office, 300 East 44th St., New York City, N.Y. 10017.**
3. ***"Saḥīḥ Al-Bukhārī"*, Arabic text and translation of the meanings, Dr. Muḥammad Muḥsin Khān,**
4. ***"Islām in Focus"*, Ḥammūdah 'Abd Al-'Āṭī, American Trust Publications, 10900 W. Washington Street, Indianapolis, IN 46231, U.S.A., 1977.**
5. ***"Towards Understanding Islām"*, Syed 'Abul A'lā Maudūdī, The ISNA Islāmic Book Service, P.O.Box 38, Plainfield, IN 46168, U.S.A., 1977.**
6. ***"Islām, The Misunderstood Religion"*, Muḥammad Quṭb Kuwait, I.I.F.S.O., 1977.**

7. *"Introduction to Islām"*, Muḥammad Ḥamīdullāh, Sh. Muhammad Ashraf Publishers, 7-Aibak Road (New Anarkali), Lahore (7), Pakistan, 1983.

8. *"The Religion of Islām"*, Sayyid Q̱uṭb, Kuwait, I.I.F.S.O., 1977.

9. *"The Family Structure in Islām"*, Ḥammūdah 'Abd Al-'Āṭī, American Trust Publications, 10900 W. Washington Street, Indianapolis, IN 46231, U.S.A., 1977.

10. *"The Lawful and the Prohibited in Islām"*, Yūsuf Al-Q̱araḏhāwī, American Trust Publications, 10900 W. Washington Street, Indianapolis, IN 46231, U.S.A.

11. *"Muḥammad in the Bible"*, Jamāl Badawī, Islāmic Information Foundation, 8 Laurel Lane, Halifax, N.S. Canada, B3M 2P6.

12. *"Christ in Islām"*, Aḥmed Deedat, Islāmic Propagation Centre International, 45/47/49 Madressa Arcade, Durban 4001, Republic of South Africa.

13. *"Islāmic Dietary Laws and Practices"*, M. M. Ḥussaini and A. Ḥ. Ṣaqr, Islāmic Food and Nutrition Council of America, P.O.Box 25407, Chicago, IL 60625, U.S.A., 1984.

14. *"Islām on Alcohol"*, Aḥmad Ḥ. Ṣaqr, Foundation for Islāmic Knowledge, P.O.Box 665, Lombard, IL 60148, U.S.A.

15. *"The Message of the Q̱ur'ān"*, Muḥammad Asad, Dar Al-Andalus, Gibraltar, 1980.

16. *"The Marital Relationships in Islām"*, Ḥussein Khālid Al-Ḥussein, MCA of the San Francisco Bay Area, 1755 Catherine St., Santa Clara, CA 95050, U.S.A., 1987.

17. *"Women In Islām"*, Ḥussein Khālid Al-Ḥussein, MCA of the San Francisco Bay Area, 1755 Catherine St., Santa Clara, CA 95050, U.S.A., 1987.

18. *"Muslim Youth in North America: Problems and Solutions"*, Ḥussein Khālid Al-Ḥussein, MCA of the San Francisco Bay Area, 1755 Catherine St., Santa Clara, CA 95050, U.S.A., 1987.